DISCLAIMER:

This book provides content related to gratitude, self-love, acceptance, and inner balance. The use of this book implies your acceptance of this disclaimer.

It would be best to note that the information in this document is for casual reading and entertainment purposes only. This book details the author's personal experiences and opinions about practicing more self-love until it was initially published. The author and publisher do not represent or warrant that the information accessible via this book is accurate, complete, or current.

We have attempted to provide accurate, up-to-date, and reliable information. However, we do not express or imply guarantees of any kind. The persons who read admit that the writer is not giving legal, financial, medical, or other advice. We put this book content by sourcing various places.

While we firmly believe that the following strategies presented in this book can positively impact your inner balance and relationship with the self, the publisher and the author make no guarantees concerning the level of success you may experience by following the advice and strategies contained in this book. You accept the risk that results differ for each individual and depend on many factors, including (but not limited to)your level of commitment to the recommendations, your baseline genetics, and your willingness to commit.

Please consult a licensed professional before trying any techniques shown in this book. By going through this document, the book reader comes to an agreement that under no situation is the author accountable for any forfeiture, direct or indirect, which they may incur because of the use of material contained in this document, including, but not limited to, errors, omissions, or inaccuracies.

THIS BOOK BELONGS TO :

- -

- -

HAPPY EASTER

HAPPY EASTER!

Easter

EGG HUNT

happy Easter

How Can You Pay It Forward?

I've put much effort into creating this coloring book, and I hope it helps your kids to have some good old fun coloring those cute easter-themed images.

If you want to make a difference, it would mean a lot to me to share your feedback with me. I'm always eager to learn new things and improve my skills.

So it would support me immensely if you could do this.

WAIT!

I HAVE A GIFT FOR YOU!

Also, it is my pleasure to offer you a Thank You for choosing my book an extra **20 Easter Egg Coloring Pages**, a resource that I hope will bring further joy to your kids. You can also share it with your friends and family.

Please drop me an email with the subject **Easter Coloring Book for Kids age 1-4** at:

 susanmay.books@gmail.com

to receive the free coloring pages and share your feedback with me.

With love,
Susan

MORE CUTE BUNNIES, AMUSING EASTER EGGS & PLAYFUL SPRING DESIGNS MEAN MORE FUN!

Discover my NEW

EASTER COLORING BOOK FOR KIDS!
&
EASTER EGG COLORING BOOK FOR KIDS AGES 1-4

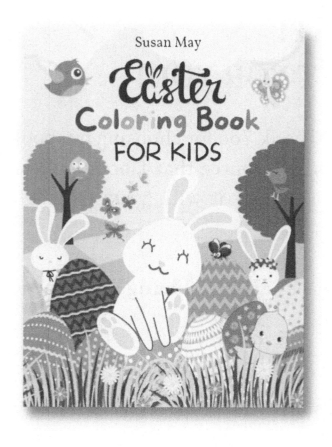

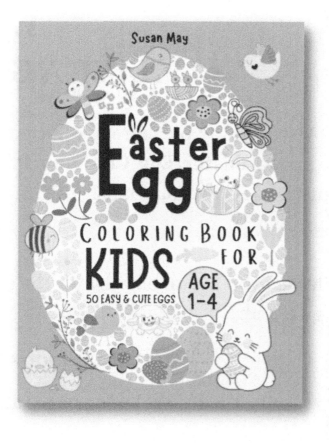

Made in the USA
Monee, IL
08 April 2022